PREPARING THE MIND OF KIDS FOR RAMADAN

BY ELIAS SULAIMON

INTRODUCTION

In this book, we will delve deep into the labyrinthine corridors of the soul, exploring the myriad ways in which we can prepare our children—physically, emotionally, and spiritually—for the rigors of fasting. From practical tips on ensuring they are physically ready to embark on this sacred journey to making Ramadan a joyous and fulfilling experience for young minds, As the crescent moon rises and the call to prayer echoes through the stillness of the night, we gather around the table of contentment, preparing to embark on a voyage of spiritual awakening and profound transformation. But beware, dear readers, for this journey is not for the faint of heart. It is a path fraught with challenges, trials, and examinations—a path where every step taken is a testament to our strength, resilience, and unwavering commitment to nurturing the young hearts. Each pages is imbued with the wisdom of ages past and the promise of a brighter future.

Together, we will bathed in the radiant light of Allah's mercy and grace. For it is in the nurturing of young hearts that we find our greatest purpose, our truest calling, and our deepest fulfillment.

"O you who have believed, protect yourselves and your families from a Fire whose fuel is people and stones, over which are [appointed] angels, harsh and severe; they do not disobey Allah in what He commands them but do what they are commanded."(Tahrim verse 6)

This verse emphasizes the responsibility of believers to not only protect themselves but also their families from the punishment of Hellfire. By calling our children to the way of Allah, we strive to guide them towards righteousness and protect them from the consequences of straying from the path of faith.

TABLE OF CONTENTS

CHAPTER ONE

NURTURING THE YOUNG HEARTS TOWARDS RAMADAN

Believers! Fasting is enjoined upon you, as it was enjoined upon those before you, that you become God-fearing. (2:183).

"When the month of Ramadan begins, the gate of the heaven are opened and the gate of hell fire are closed and the shaytan and his companions are chained." (buhkari)

1. **Helping kids grasp the essence of Ramadan nurtures their spiritual development. It's a chance for them to learn about fasting, prayer, and self-reflection in Islam. Ramadan holds immense significance in Islamic culture, weaving into its rich tapestry. Teaching children about Ramadan aids in their cultural connection, acquainting them with its customs and traditions. During Ramadan, communities thrive with increased interaction—attending mosque prayers, engaging in charitable deeds, and relishing meals with loved ones. Engaging kids in these experiences fosters a sense of belonging and instills values of togetherness and kindness within them.**

2. **Nurturing the young hearts towards Ramadan involves fostering a deep understanding and appreciation of the spiritual significance of this sacred month. It begins with education, teaching**

children about the virtues of Ramadan, such as patience, empathy, and self-discipline. Parents and educators can create a nurturing environment by engaging children in age-appropriate discussions about fasting, prayer, and acts of charity.

3. Leading by example is essential; parents and caregivers should demonstrate sincerity in their observance of Ramadan, showing children the importance of devotion and spiritual growth. Encouraging children to participate in Ramadan rituals, such as breaking fast together as a family and attending taraweeh prayers, helps instill a sense of belonging and community.

4. Involvement fostering a deep connection to Allah and His teachings, guiding children to develop a strong spiritual foundation that will last beyond the month of Ramadan and throughout their lives.

5. **Cooking together Involve children in the kitchen to prepare special Ramadan recipes. This not only teaches them about traditional foods associated with Ramadan but also provides an opportunity for bonding and creating cherished memories.**

6. **Education teaches children about the significance of Ramadan in Islam, its history, and the importance of fasting as one of the Five Pillars of Islam.**

7. **Lead by example by demonstrating devotion to prayers, fasting, and acts of charity during Ramadan.**

8. **Introduce children to the concept of Ramadan at a young age, gradually explaining its significance as they grow older.**

9. Involve children in Ramadan preparations such as meal planning, decorating the house, and organizing charitable activities.

10. Share stories and anecdotes about Ramadan and its significance in an engaging and age-appropriate manner.

CHAPTER TWO

BE ASURE THEY ARE PHYSICALLY READY TO FAST

For those who are capable of fasting (but still do not fast) there is a redemption: feeding a needy man for each day missed. Whoever voluntarily does more good than is required, will find it better for him and that you should fast is better for you. (Surah Al Baqarah Ayat 184)

The Messenger of Allah (ﷺ) said, "The one who is proficient in the recitation of the Qur'an will be with the honorable and obedient scribes (angels) and he who recites the Qur'an and finds it difficult to recite, doing his best to recite it in the best way possible, will have two rewards." [Al-Bukhari and Muslim].

1. Encourage children to maintain healthy eating habits during non-fasting hours. Emphasize the

importance of consuming nutritious foods that provide sustained energy, such as fruits, vegetables, whole grains, and lean proteins.

2. Ensure that children drink plenty of fluids, especially during non-fasting hours, to stay hydrated. Encourage them to drink water, milk, and natural fruit juices rather than sugary or caffeinated beverages.

3. Make sure children get enough rest and sleep to support their overall health and well-being. Establish a consistent bedtime routine and encourage relaxation techniques to help them unwind and recharge.

4. Encourage children to engage in moderate physical activity during Ramadan, but advise them to avoid

strenuous exercise, especially during fasting hours. Encourage activities that promote gentle movement, such as walking, yoga, or light stretching.

5. Keep a close eye on children's physical health throughout Ramadan. Watch for signs of fatigue, dehydration, or other health concerns, and seek medical attention if needed.

6. Provide children with encouragement and support as they fast during Ramadan. Let them know that it's okay to break their fast if they feel unwell or if fasting poses a risk to their health. Reinforce the importance of listening to their bodies and prioritizing their well-being, parents can help ensure that children are physically prepared for fasting during Ramadan, promoting a safe and healthy fasting experience.

7. Preparing children for Ramadan, particularly in terms of physical readiness, involves a combination of ensuring they have a balanced diet, maintaining hydration, getting adequate rest, and gradually introducing them to the changes in routine that Ramadan brings. Here are some tips:

8. Let children approach Ramadan with mindfulness and intentionality. Focus on the spiritual growth and purification it offers, and strive to make the most of this blessed month.

9. Make sure your children eat a wholesome suhoor meal before the fast begins. Include foods that release energy slowly, such as complex carbohydrates (whole grains), proteins (eggs, dairy, nuts), and healthy fats (avocado, olive oil). This will

help them feel fuller for longer during the fasting hours.

10. It's essential for children to stay hydrated, especially during the non-fasting hours. Encourage them to drink plenty of water between iftar (breaking fast) and suhoor. Avoid caffeinated drinks like tea and coffee as they can lead to dehydration.

11. Limit physical exertion during the fasting hours, it's advisable for children to avoid strenuous physical activities, especially outdoor activities in hot weather. Instead, encourage lighter exercises and activities that are less demanding.

CHAPTER THREE

HOW TO MAKE RAMADAN EASY AND SIMPLE FOR KIDS

Make sure they are healthy and sounding, I will suggest you take them to the hospital for a checkup to confirm their healthy status and enable them an access to physical exercise.

Why does Allah want us to fast in Ramadan?
The purpose of fasting is to develop the quality of righteousness (taqwa) by abstaining from sinful deeds and training ourselves to control our day. Allah Almighty says,

(O you who believe! Ward yourselves and your families off from a fire (Hell) whose fuel is of men and stones, over which are appointed angels stern and severe, who do not disobey the commands they receive from Allah, and execute that which they are commanded.) (Tahrim)

1. Celebrate children's achievements and efforts during Ramadan, whether it's completing their first fast, memorizing a new surah from the Quran, or performing acts of charity. Acknowledge their accomplishments and praise their dedication and commitment.

   By implementing these strategies, parents and caregivers can make Ramadan a positive and enriching experience for children, fostering a love for the month and its teachings that will stay with them for years to come.

2. Focus on the Spirit of Ramadan: Instead of solely focusing on the rules and obligations of fasting, emphasize the spiritual essence of Ramadan, such as developing empathy, gratitude, patience, and compassion. Teach children the importance of using this month as an opportunity for self-reflection and self-improvement.

3. Let them participate in physical activities, watch Islamic TV, play with their friends, and provide them with halal toys. Toys can be a helpful distraction from food cravings and fasting struggles.

4. Motivate them to persevere through the day, even if they may struggle to make it to iftar. Promise them the reward of delicious fruits and drinks at iftar to keep them motivated. Allah urges believers to protect themselves and their families from the fire of Hell (Surat At-Tahrim).

5. Understand that children may have days when they struggle with fasting or may not be able to participate fully due to other commitments or health reasons. Be flexible and supportive, and encourage them to do their best without putting undue pressure on them.

6. Ease into Ramadan by gradually adjusting your child's eating and sleeping routines a few weeks beforehand. This helps their bodies adapt to the changes in meal times and sleep patterns. Stay flexible and understanding. Recognize that fasting might be challenging for children at times. If they feel unwell or excessively hungry, allow them to break their fast and make it up later.

7. Generosity (Sakhawat) Be generous with your time, resources, and kindness towards others, especially those in need.

8. Forgive those who have wronged them and seek forgiveness from others for any wrongdoings. Maintain humility in their actions and interactions, avoiding arrogance or pride.

CHAPTER FOUR

CHARACTER AND CONDUCT WITH GOOD MANERS IN THE MONTH OF RAMADAN

1. **Muslim children should treat others with kindness and respect, just as they would like to be treated. This includes giving gifts, wearing a smile, sharing love, showing compassion, and responding to negativity with kindness. Positive character traits cultivated through fasting include valuing time, respecting others' rights, honesty, patience, and generosity towards those in need, including parents when they require assistance.**

   "And fear a Day when no soul will suffice for another soul at all, nor will intercession be accepted from it, nor will compensation be taken from it, nor will they be aided." (See Baqarah verse 123)

2. **Make sure your children perform all their daily prayers without missing any during Ramadan. Prayer is crucial**

during and after Ramadan, so guide and ensure they understand its significance.

3. Teach your children the importance of respecting elders, peers, and authority figures, as well as respecting cultural and religious customs not only during Ramadan but always.

4. Encourage children to be gracious and polite in their interactions with others. Teach them to say "please" and "thank you," greet others with a smile, and show appreciation for acts of kindness and generosity. By emphasizing these values and teachings, parents and educators can help children develop strong character, conduct, and good manners during the month of Ramadan and beyond, laying the foundation for a life guided by Islamic principles and ethics.

5. Honesty and Integrity: Teach children the value of honesty and integrity in all aspects of their lives. Encourage them to speak the truth, keep their promises,

and act with sincerity and integrity in their interactions with others.

6. Self-Discipline: Ramadan is an opportunity to develop self-discipline and self-control. Encourage children to refrain from negative behaviors such as gossiping, lying, or arguing, and instead focus on positive actions that align with Islamic teachings.

CHAPTER FIVE

GIVING AND CHARITY TIPS FOR KIDS

"By no means shall ye attain righteousness unless ye give (freely) of that which ye love; and whatever you give, of a truth God Know it well" (surah al-'imran 3:92)

1.   Encourage your children's natural instinct to help others by engaging them in charitable activities. Allow them to choose a charity to support and assist them in setting aside money for donation. You can also motivate them to volunteer their time for a charitable cause.

2.   Teach your child the importance of giving by allocating a portion of their allowance or savings to assist those in need during Ramadan. Remember, it's the act of giving that holds significance, not the amount.

3.   Share with your children the significance of Ramadan as a time for spiritual reflection and generosity

towards others. Stress the importance Muslims place on charity during Ramadan as a means of seeking blessings and forgiveness from Allah.

4.   Instill integrity in your children by highlighting the value of honesty, sincerity, and moral principles in all their actions, regardless of whether someone is watching or not.

5.   Nurture gratitude in your children by helping them recognize that not everyone enjoys the same privileges they do. Encourage them to contemplate their blessings and ponder how they can contribute to improving the world through acts of kindness and compassion.

6. Participate in online charity campaigns Support online charity campaigns or fundraisers by sharing them on social media or making donations together as a family.

7. Read stories or watch videos about charitable acts and discuss them with children to inspire and motivate them in doing goods.

6. Encourage children to express gratitude for their blessings by making dua (supplication) for those in need during their prayers.

7. Take time to reflect with children on the impact of their charitable actions and the positive difference they are making in the lives of others.

8. Help children understand the concept of sacrifice by encouraging them to give up something they enjoy, such as a favorite treat or toy, and donate the money saved to charity.

CHAPTER SIX

ENCOURAGING THEM IN THE REMEMBRANCE OF ALLAH

"Men who remember Allah standing, sitting and lying down on their sides and contemplate the (wonders of) creation." (3:191)

1. Use physical rewards to motivate your children to read the Quran. Consider small gifts like colorful pencils, specific candies, or items they desire. Regularly reward them for their progress, whether it's after memorizing a surah or a combination of surahs. Promising these rewards will incentivize your children to complete the task.

2. Encourage your children to engage in their azkar by teaching the essential daily supplications, both during Ramadan and throughout the year. E.g "LA ILAHA ILLALLAH, WAHDAHU LASHARIKA LAH, LAHU L-MULK WALAHUL-HAMD WAHUWA ALA KULLI SHAY'IN QADIR."

3. Establish a family routine of Quran recitation. Dedicate a specific time each day to gather as a family and recite

together. Encourage your child to take turns leading the recitation, even if it's just a few verses. Additionally, expose them to recordings of renowned reciters like Sheikh As-Sudais, El Minshawy, Abdul Basit, Mustofa Ismail, and the likes.

4. Instill hope and optimism in your children by exposing them to the comforting and uplifting messages of the Quran. Encouraging Quran reading during Ramadan can inspire resilience and a positive outlook on life's challenges.

5. Promote a sense of community by participating in Quran recitations and study circles with your family and local community during Ramadan. These activities foster a sense of belonging and connection to the wider Muslim community.

6. Organize dhikr sessions, where everyone gathers to engage in remembrance collectively. This could be after prayer times, before bedtime, or during family gatherings.

7. Help children develop a habit of reflecting on Allah's blessings and expressing gratitude for them. Encourage them to recognize and appreciate the countless favors Allah has bestowed upon them.

7. Reward and praise their efforts by acknowledge and praise them when they actively participate in dhikr or show interest in learning about their faith. Offer simple rewards or incentives to reinforce positive behavior and motivate them to continue.

8. Create a supportive environment: Foster an atmosphere of love, encouragement, and positivity around the practice of dhikr. Avoid making it feel like a chore or obligation; instead, emphasize the joy and blessings that come from remembering Allah. By incorporating these strategies into your parenting approach, you can help instill a love for the remembrance of Allah in your children and nurture their spiritual growth from a young age.

CHAPTER SEVEN

SHOWING THEM THE KINDNESS AND CHARITY

1. Visit homeless shelters provide vital support to individuals experiencing homelessness. You can visit any homeless shelters in your area to volunteer your time, offer assistance, or donate items such as food, clothing, and toiletries.

2. Food banks and shelters are always in need of volunteers and donations, especially during Ramadan when there may be an increased demand for assistance. Consider visiting your local food bank or shelter to volunteer your time or donate food, clothing, or other essential items.

3. Explain to your children that Ramadan is a time for spiritual reflection and giving to others. Emphasize that Muslims view charity during Ramadan as essential for seeking blessings and forgiveness from Allah.

4. Foster integrity in children by emphasizing the importance of honesty, sincerity, and moral values in all their actions, even when nobody is watching.

5. Visiting prisons during Ramadan to advocate for reforms in the criminal justice system, including efforts to promote rehabilitation, reduce recidivism, and support the rights and dignity of prisoners.

Visiting prisons during Ramadan requires sensitivity, compassion, and respect for the dignity of inmates. By offering your time, resources, and support, you can make a meaningful difference in the lives of incarcerated individuals during this sacred month

6. Send Care Packages to Orphanages: Prepare care packages with essentials and treats for children in orphanages or foster care, brightening their day and showing them they are loved.

7. Visiting hospitals with children before and during Ramadan can be a compassionate and charitable act, especially considering that there may be patients who are fasting or are in need of support during this time. Many patients in hospitals may feel lonely or isolated, particularly during holidays like Ramadan. Your visit can provide comfort and companionship to patients, offering them emotional support and a sense of connection during their time of need.

8. Donate Blood: If eligible, donate blood as a family to help save lives and support those in need of transfusions or medical treatment.

9. Encourage children to express gratitude for their blessings by keeping a gratitude journal or reflecting on the things they are thankful for each day.

CHAPTER EIGHT

THE BENEFITS AND THE REWARDS OF ALLAH FOR THE SOOYIM

Prophet Muhammad (peace be upon him) said, "He who fasts Ramadan with faith and seeks its reward from Allah, will have his past sins forgiven." (Sahih Bukhari)

1. Fasting from dawn to dusk facilitates the body's natural detoxification process, helping expel toxins and regulate metabolism. It's not just about food intake but also about cultivating patience and perseverance, which contribute to maintaining overall health.

2. Fasting during Ramadan is a fundamental pillar of Islam, signifying submission to Allah's commandments. It fosters humility and empathy as we experience hunger and thirst, allowing us to empathize with the less fortunate and appreciate Allah's blessings. This empathy motivates us to support those in need.

3. Ramadan is the month when the Qur'an was revealed, and Muslims honor this by engaging deeply with its

teachings. Through recitation, memorization, listening, and studying its exegesis, believers strengthen their connection with the Qur'an. Completing its recitation during this sacred month holds great spiritual reward.

4. Muslims believe that prayers made during Ramadan, especially on Laylat al-Qadr (the Night of Decree), are more likely to be answered by Allah. This belief instills a sense of hope and devotion, encouraging believers to make heartfelt supplications throughout the month. In summary, fasting in Ramadan transcends mere physical discipline; it's a pathway to spiritual growth and devotion. The promised rewards from Allah for sincere fasting serve as motivation for Muslims to embrace the blessings of this sacred month fully.

5. Developing Empathy: Experiencing hunger and thirst during fasting fosters empathy towards the less fortunate and increases compassion for those who are struggling with poverty and hunger.

6. Increasing Spiritual Awareness: Fasting heightens one's spiritual awareness and connection to Allah, making it easier to engage in acts of worship such as prayer, Quranic recitation, and remembrance of Allah.

7. Increased Taqwa (God-consciousness): Fasting instills a sense of piety and consciousness of Allah, as individuals strive to obey His commands and avoid sins during the fasting period.

8. Fasting is considered a means of seeking forgiveness for past sins. It is believed that Allah forgives the sins of those who fast sincerely and with devotion.

9. Fasting elevates the status of believers in the sight of Allah. It is mentioned in a Hadith that Allah says, "Every deed of the son of Adam is for him, except fasting; it is for me, and I shall reward for it. Forgiveness of sins: Fasting is considered a means of seeking forgiveness for past sins. It is believed that Allah forgives the sins of those who fast sincerely and with devotion.

10. Fasting fosters empathy and compassion towards the less fortunate by experiencing hunger and thirst firsthand. It encourages believers to be more charitable and generous towards those in need.

Overall, fasting in Islam is not just about abstaining from food and drink; it encompasses a holistic approach to spiritual growth, self-discipline, and moral refinement, with the promise of abundant rewards and blessings from Allah for those who observe it sincerely.

CHAPTER NINE

DESIRABILITY OF GOING TO PRAYER WITH DIGNITY AND TRANQUILLITY AND FORBIDDANCE THEM OF GOING TO IT IN HOT HASTE

1.   Abu Huraira reported: I heard the Messenger of Allah (may peace be upon him) saying: When the Iqama has been pronounced for prayer, do not go running to it, but go walking in tranquility and pray what you are in time for, and complete what you have missed.

2.   Abu Huraira reported that the Messenger of Allah (may peace be upon him) said: When the words of Iqama are pronounced, do not come to (prayer) running, but go with tranquility, and pray what you are in time for, and complete (what you have missed) for when one of you is preparing for prayer he is in fact engaged in prayer.

CHAPTER TEN

QUIZ FOR KIDS

1. Who is the first prophet in Islam?

Adam B) Moses C) Jesus D) Muhammad

Answer: A) Adam

2. What is the holy book of Islam?

Bible B) Quran C) Torah D) Tripitaka

Answer: B) Quran

3. What is the name of the angel who brought messages from Allah to the prophets?

Gabriel B) Michael C) Raphael D) Uriel

Answer: A) Gabriel

4. What is the capital city of Saudi Arabia? A) Cairo B) Dubai C) Riyadh D) Istanbul

Answer: C) Riyadh

5. What is the name of the month of fasting in Islam? A) Ramadan B) Shawwal C) Dhul-Hijjah D) Muharram

Answer: A) Ramadan

6. How many times a day do Muslims pray? A) Two B) Three C) Four D) Five

Answer: D) Five

7. What is the pilgrimage to Mecca called? A) Hajj B) Umrah C) Eid D) Shahada

Answer: A) Hajj

8. What is the name of the Muslim place of worship? A) Temple B) Church C) Mosque D) Synagogue

Answer: C) Mosque

9. Which prophet built the Kaaba? A) Abraham B) Moses C) Jesus D) Muhammad

Answer: A) Abraham

10. What is the name of the first wife of Prophet Muhammad? A) Aisha B) Khadijah C) Fatimah D) Hafsah

Answer: B) Khadijah

11. How many pillars of Islam are there? A) Three B) Four C) Five D) Six

Answer: C) Five

12. What is the Islamic greeting? A) Peace be upon you B) Good morning C) Hello D) Namaste

Answer: A) Peace be upon you

13. Who was the first Caliph of Islam? A) Abu Bakr B) Umar C) Uthman D) Ali

Answer: A) Abu Bakr

14. What is the significance of the month of Muharram? A) Ramadan begins B) Prophet Muhammad was born C) Battle of Badr took place D) Ashura, the day of fasting and reflection, occurs

Answer: D) Ashura, the day of fasting and reflection, occurs in

15. In which city was Prophet Muhammad born? A) Mecca B) Medina C) Jerusalem D) Cairo

 Answer: A) Mecca

16. What is the name of the Islamic declaration of faith? A) Dua B) Surah C) Shahada D) Adhan

 Answer: C) Shahada

17. What is the significance of the month of Shawwal? A) Eid al-Fitr is celebrated B) Ramadan begins C) Hajj pilgrimage takes place D) Prophet Muhammad was born

 Answer: A) Eid al-Fitr is celebrated

18. What is the name of the Islamic law? A) Sharia B) Halal C) Sunnah D) Hadith

 Answer: A) Sharia

19. Who was the first martyr in Islam? A) Ali B) Abu Bakr C) Umar D) Sumayyah bint Khabbab

Answer: D) Sumayyah bint Khabbab

20. Which direction do Muslims face when praying? A) North B) South C) East D) West

Answer: C) East

21. Who was the last prophet in Islam? A) Abraham B) Moses C) Jesus D) Muhammad

Answer: D) Muhammad

22. What is the name of the night journey of Prophet Muhammad from Mecca to Jerusalem? A) Hijrah B) Isra C) Laylat al-Qadr D) Taqwa

Answer: B) Isra

23. What is the name of the Islamic month during which fasting is obligatory? A) Shawwal B) Dhul-Hijjah C) Rajab D) Ramadan

Answer: D) Ramadan

24. Who was the first woman to accept Islam? A) Khadijah B) Fatimah C) Aisha D) Hafsah

Answer: A) Khadijah

25. Which prophet is often referred to as "Khalilullah" in Islam? A) Moses B) Jesus C) Abraham D) Solomon

Answer: C) Abraham

26. Which animal did Prophet Muhammad ride during the Isra and Mi'raj? A) Horse B) Camel C) Elephant D) Buraq

Answer: D) Buraq

27. What is the meaning of the word "Islam"? A) Peace B) Submission C) Love D) Mercy

Answer: B) Submission

28. How many days are there in the Islamic lunar calendar? A) 365 B) 354 C) 366 D) 360

Answer: B) 354

29. Who was the first child to accept Islam? A) Ali B) Fatimah C) Abu Bakr D) Zayd ibn Harithah

Answer: D) Zayd ibn Harithah

30. What is the name of the Islamic month during which Hajj is performed? A) Ramadan B) Dhul-Hijjah C) Shawwal D) Safar

Answer: B) Dhul-Hijjah

31. What is the name of the Islamic prayer leader? A) Muezzin B) Imam C) Sheikh D) Hafiz

Answer: B) Imam

32. What is the significance of the month of Rabi' al-Awwal? A) Ramadan begins B) Eid al-Fitr is celebrated C) Prophet Muhammad was born D) Hajj pilgrimage takes place

Answer: C) Prophet Muhammad was born

33. What is the name of the well from which Prophet Muhammad used to get water in Mecca? A) Zamzam B) Arafat C) Safa D) Marwa

Answer: A) Zamzam

34. Which city is known as the city of the Prophet in Islam?
A) Mecca B) Medina C) Jerusalem D) Damascus

Answer: B) Medina

35. What is the name of the Islamic month during which fasting is forbidden? A) Shawwal B) Dhul-Hijjah C) Rajab D) Muharram

Answer: B) Dhul-Hijjah

36. Who was the first martyr of the Battle of Uhud? A) Hamza B) Ali C) Abu Bakr D) Mus'ab ibn Umayr

Answer: D) Mus'ab ibn Umayr

37. What is the name of the angel who will blow the trumpet on the Day of Judgment? A) Gabriel B) Michael C) Israfil D) Azrael

Answer: C) Israfil

38. What is the name of the angel of death in Islam? A) Gabriel B) Michael C) Israfil D) Azrael

Answer: D) Azrael

39. What is the Islamic month during which fasting can be made up for missed days of Ramadan? A) Shawwal B) Dhul-Hijjah C) Rajab D) Sha'ban

Answer: A) Shawwal

40. What is the name of the Prophet's mosque in Medina? A) Masjid al-Haram B) Masjid al-Aqsa C) Masjid al-Nabawi D) Masjid Quba

Answer: C) Masjid al-Nabawi

41. Who was the first woman to lead an Islamic battle? A) Khadijah B) Fatimah C) Aisha D) Umm Salamah

Answer: C) Aisha

42. What is the Islamic ruling on eating pork? A) Permissible B) Discouraged C) Forbidden D) Recommended

Answer: C) Forbidden

43. What is the name of the Islamic month during which fasting is highly recommended but not obligatory? A) Shawwal B) Dhul-Hijjah C) Rajab D) Sha'ban

Answer: D) Sha'ban

44. What is the significance of the month of Rajab? A) Ramadan begins B) Hajj pilgrimage takes place C) Isra and Mi'raj occurred D) Battle of Badr took place

Answer: C) Isra and Mi'raj occurred

45. Who was the first woman to accept Islam after Khadijah? A) Fatimah B) Aisha C) Umm Salamah D) Asma bint Abu Bakr

Answer: C) Umm Salamah

46. What is the name of the angel who records the deeds of humans? A) Gabriel B) Michael C) Israfil D) Kiraman Katibin

Answer: D) Kiraman Katibin

47. What is the name of the Islamic month during which the Quran was first revealed? A) Shawwal B) Dhul-Hijjah C) Rajab D) Ramadan

Answer: D) Ramadan

48. What is the significance of the month of Safar? A) Ramadan begins B) Hajj pilgrimage takes place C) Battle of Badr took place D) No significant events

 Answer: D) No significant events

49. Who was the first martyr in Islam? A) Ali B) Abu Bakr C) Umar D) Sumayyah bint Khabbab

 Answer: D) Sumayyah bint Khabbab

50. What is the name of the pilgrimage performed outside the Hajj season? A) Hajj al-Akbar B) Hajj al-Asghar C) Umrah D) Tawaf

Answer: C) Umar

CONCLUSION

This guidebook offers a comprehensive approach to preparing children for Ramadan. From nurturing young hearts towards Ramadan to ensuring they are physically ready to fast, each chapter provides valuable insights and practical tips. Parents are guided on making Ramadan enjoyable and simple for kids, fostering good character and conduct, and teaching them about giving and charity. Encouragement in remembering Allah and engaging in prayers, along with demonstrating kindness and charity, are emphasized. The book also explores the benefits and rewards of fasting and teaches children the etiquette of the mosque through relevant Hadith.